Let's go to

SRI LANKA

Dhanapala Samarasekara

General Editor

Henry Pluckrose

Franklin Watts

London   New York   Sydney   Toronto

F

Facts about Sri Lanka

Area:
65,610 sq. km.
(25,332 sq. miles)

Population:
15,416,000

Capital:
Colombo

Largest cities:
Colombo (602,000)
Dehiwela-Mt Lavinia
(near Colombo, 177,000)
Moratuwa (near Colombo,
136,000)
Jaffna (121,000)
Kandy (107,000)

Official language:
Sinhala

Religions:
Buddhism, Hinduism,
Islam, Christianity

Main exports:
Tea, textiles, rubber,
coconut products, precious
and semi-precious stones

Currency:
Rupee

Franklin Watts
12a Golden Square
London W1

Franklin Watts Inc.
387 Park Avenue South
New York, N.Y. 10016

ISBN: UK Edition 0 86313 500 5
ISBN: US Edition 0 531 10288 2
Library of Congress Catalog Card No:
86 50898

© Franklin Watts Limited 1987

Maps: Susan Kinsey and Simon
Roulestone
Design: Edward Kinsey
Stamps: Stanley Gibbons
Photographs: Paul Forrester 10; Polly
Lyster 4, 27, 32; Rex Features 7; Sri
Lankan Tourist Office 58, 12, 13, 17, 20,
21, 23, 24, 25, 28, 29, 30, 31; ZEFA 3, 6,
9, 14, 15, 16, 18, 19, 22
Front Cover: Sri Lankan Tourist Board
Back Cover: Sri Lankan Tourist Board

Typeset by Ace Filmsetting Ltd
Frome, Somerset
Printed in Hong Kong

Sri Lanka is an island country off the southeast coast of India. It was once called Ceylon. Sri Lanka is about the size of the Republic of Ireland. It has many beautiful beaches, such as here at Trincomalee in the northeast. It has a warm, tropical climate.

Six main groups of people live in Sri Lanka. The largest group, the Sinhalese, make up about 74 percent of the population. Their ancestors came to Sri Lanka from northern India in about 500 BC. A few Veddas, the descendants of early peoples, still live in remote areas.

Most Sinhalese are Buddhists. The Buddha, the founder of Buddhism who lived between about 563 and 483 BC, is believed to have visited Sri Lanka three times. Anuradhapura, in the north, was the Sinhalese capital from the 4th century BC to the 11th century AD. It has many shrines.

Tamils make up about 19 percent of the population. Their ancestors came from southern India. Most Tamils are Hindus. This Hindu temple is in Trincomalee. Between the 12th and 16th centuries, Tamils ruled the north, with their capital in Jaffna. The Sinhalese ruled the south.

The ancestors of about two thirds of the Tamils came to Sri Lanka in ancient times. Some Tamils want to preserve their own culture and language. The differences between them and the Sinhalese have led to some clashes.

The ancestors of about a third of the Tamils came to Sri Lanka in recent times. Many of these so called "Indian Tamils" work on tea and rubber estates. Nearly eight percent of Sri Lanka's people are Muslims. They include Moors, the descendants of Arabs, and Malays.

The Portuguese landed in Colombo, now Sri Lanka's capital, in 1505. The Dutch took over parts of the island in 1656. The British replaced them in 1796. Britain ruled until 1948. The Europeans introduced Christianity. The descendants of the Portuguese and Dutch are called Burghers.

9

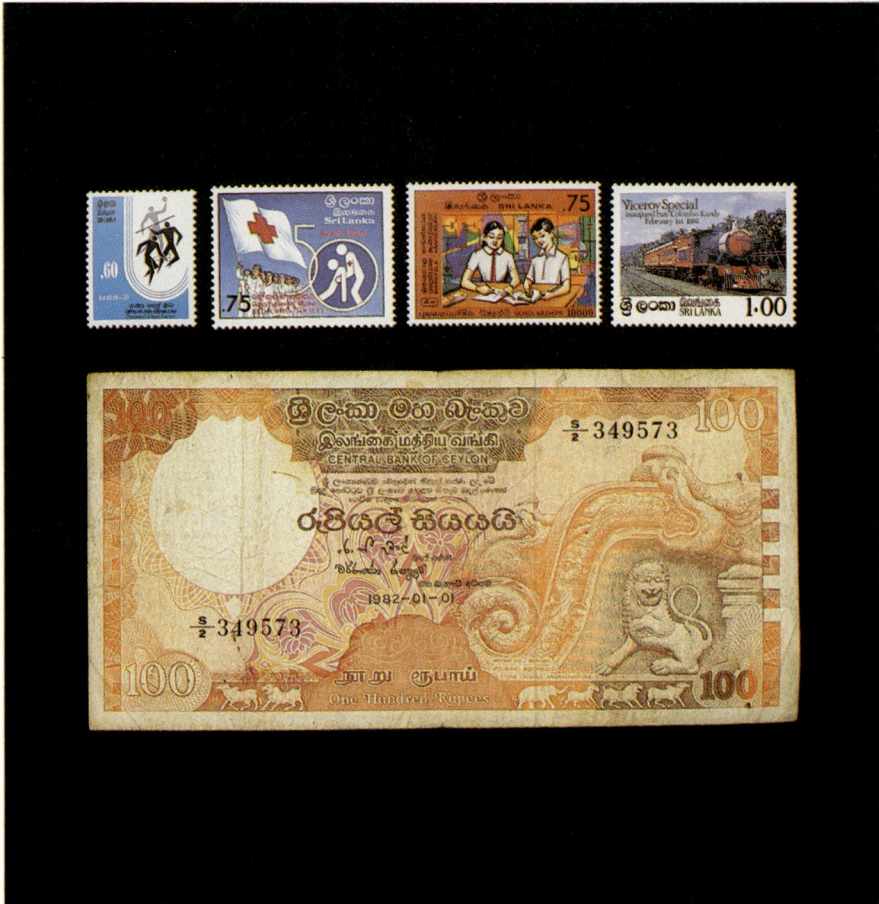

The picture shows some stamps
and money used in Sri Lanka. The
main unit of currency is the rupee,
which is divided into 100 cents.

10

Sri Lanka

Jaffna

Bay of Bengal

INDIA

Adams Bridge

Mannar

Gulf of Manaar

Trincomalee

Anuradhapura

Sigiriya

Puttalam

SRI LANKA

Batticola

Indian Ocean

Negombo

Kandy

Badulla

Colombo

Pidurutalagala 2523m

Adams Peak 2242m

Kalutara

Ratnapura

Galle

Matara

11

The country's official name is the Democratic Socialist Republic of Sri Lanka. The elected President heads the government. Parliament consists of one chamber with 168 elected members. The parliament is at Kotte, near Colombo.

Colombo, the capital, chief seaport and focus of business life in Sri Lanka, contains a mixture of old and new buildings. About 23 out of every 100 people in Sri Lanka live in cities or towns. The rest of them live in the countryside.

13

Galle on the southwest coast was a major port from ancient times. Some experts think that it once received the ships of the Biblical King Solomon. Galle declined in the 19th century, when Colombo became the chief port.

The city of Kandy is in the hilly region of south-central Sri Lanka. It contains the famous Buddhist Temple of the Tooth, where a sacred tooth said to be that of the Buddha is preserved. This tooth is Sri Lanka's most prized possession.

15

The scenic central highlands reach
a height of 2,524 m (8,281 ft). Parts
of the highlands have 3,750 mm
(148 in) of rain a year. This is nearly
four times as much as falls on the
northern plains. The heavy rainfall
swells the rivers.

16

About four fifths of Sri Lanka is less than 300 m (984 ft) above sea level. Elephants are common sights throughout the country, and are used in the logging industry. Their owners allow them to cool off after a long day's work.

Farming employs 54 out of every 100 workers in Sri Lanka. The chief food crop is rice, some of which grows on flat terraces which have been carefully built down sloping land.

Many farmers use water buffaloes to turn over the soil before they plant rice seedlings. This simple form of farming contrasts with the advanced methods used on tea estates.

Tea accounts for a third of the country's exports. Sri Lanka and India are the world's two largest tea exporters. Tea grows mostly in the uplands. Rubber, which makes up 11 percent of Sri Lanka's exports, grows mainly on lower slopes.

Coconut palms grow mostly on the coastal plains. Coconut products make up six percent of Sri Lanka's exports. They include coconut oil and the husks, which are made into rope and matting.

Freshwater and deep sea fishing are expanding in Sri Lanka. The picture shows traditional boats in the town of Negombo, north of Colombo. The fishermen here catch crabs and prawns, as well as various sea fishes.

Tourism is important and over 300,000 visitors arrive every year. They enjoy the sunny beaches, the country's rich cultural traditions, and Sri Lanka's five national parks, which contain many wild animals.

23

Sri Lanka is one of the world's top gem producers. Sediments which contain valuable stones are placed in baskets. The mud is washed away, while the heavy stones settle on the bottom. Ratnapura is the leading region for gems.

Precious and semiprecious stones account for four percent of Sri Lanka's exports. Jewellery making is an ancient industry. But many new factories are being built. They are powered by electricity produced by water power.

All education is free and schooling is compulsory from the ages of 6 to 14. The school in this picture is in Dehiwala-Mount Lavinia, a city which is very close to Colombo. Most schools are run by the government.

Cricket, soccer and volleyball are
among the leading sports in Sri
Lanka. But more light-hearted forms
of exercise, including "wheelbarrow"
races, are popular pastimes in schools.

27

Rice, the chief food in Sri Lanka, is served with curry dishes made from fish, meat and vegetables. Many people grind their own curry powder from a mixture of spices and herbs. Yoghurt is also popular.

28

Religion plays a major part in people's lives. The picture shows a family at prayer. Western clothes are common, but many women wear saris, while men often wear sarongs (cloths wrapped around the waist).

Music is a leading art form. Fast and exciting rhythms are beaten out on drums to accompany dancers who often perform acrobatic feats. Many dances have their origins in religious rites and ceremonies.

Religious processions take place in Kandy every August. A temple elephant, covered by beautiful cloth and lit by electric bulbs, carries the golden casket, which contains the sacred tooth of the Buddha.

Index

32